Terms and Conditions

LEGAL NOTICE

The Publisher has strived to be as accurate and complete as possible in the creation of this report, notwithstanding the fact that he does not warrant or represent at any time that the contents within are accurate due to the rapidly changing nature of the Internet.

While all attempts have been made to verify information provided in this publication, the Publisher assumes no responsibility for errors, omissions, or contrary interpretation of the subject matter herein. Any perceived slights of specific persons, peoples, or organizations are unintentional.

In practical advice books, like anything else in life, there are no guarantees of income made. Readers are cautioned to reply on their own judgment about their individual circumstances to act accordingly.

This book is not intended for use as a source of legal, business, accounting or financial advice. All readers are advised to seek services of competent professionals in legal, business, accounting and finance fields.

You are encouraged to print this book for easy reading.

Table Of Contents

Foreword

Chapter 1:
Introduction To Facebook

Chapter 2:
Basics Of Facebook Marketing

Chapter 3:
Building Your Online Presence Using Fanpages

Chapter 4:
Getting Opt Ins Using Facebook

Chapter 5:
Viral Power

Chapter 6:
Integrating Facebook With Other Websites

Chapter 7:
Facebook Advertising

Chapter 8:
Facebook Marketing Mistakes To Avoid

Wrapping Up

Foreword

If Facebook was a country, it would be the 3rd largest country in the world right after China and India. That is how fast Facebook is growing and is the most visited website on the planet.

If you do not tap into this massive source of traffic immediately, you would potentially be missing out of tons of new leads and traffic for your business.

This guide aims to reveal the secrets and strategies used by the top marketers to grow their online business through Facebook.

And you'll be able to easily learn and apply these strategies for yourself, no matter what niche you are in.

Excited? So am I. **Let's Get Started!**

Facebook Marketing Mania

Become The Next Social Media Mogul By Mastering Facebook Marketing

Chapter 1:

Introduction To Facebook

Synopsis

Before there was Facebook™, there were other online social networking sites such Friendster™, MySpace™ and Hi5™. Social networking sites were the next hot thing in the web 2.0 era, where not only could people pour out tons of user generated content with ease, they could share it with their "friends" or online social contacts.

Intro

As the number of users increased and the growth of Facebook boomed, so did the number of applications for Facebook. You could install apps, play games, chat and even share and upload photos to Facebook.

The business minded people began to see the potential in Facebook. They began looking into ways one can monetize or grow one's business through the Facebook platform.

Now, with over 500 million users, Facebook's potential for businesses to grow cannot be ignored. With the recent introduction of Facebook Advertising and Facebook pages, businesses can list their own official fan pages on Facebook to connect with their customers and grow their businesses.

In the next section, you'll look into the power of Facebook Marketing!

Chapter 2:

Basics Of Facebook Marketing

Synopsis

Facebook marketing is literally means using Facebook to market your business, build traffic or grow your leads. It is a branch of Social Media Marketing, where marketers tap into a multitude of social media platforms such as social networking sites, video sharing sites or micro-blogging platforms to grow their business.

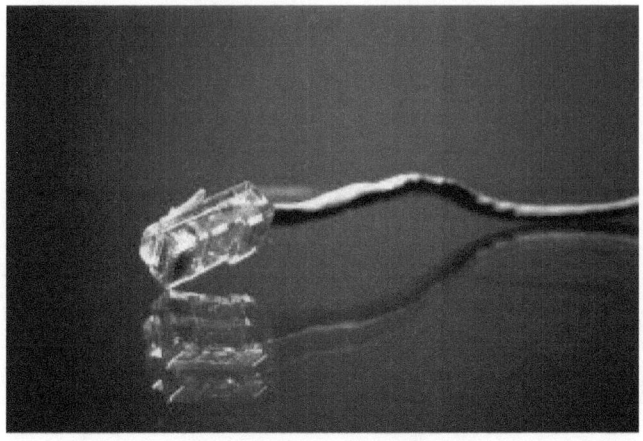

The Basics

As mentioned earlier, Facebook has a useful feature called Fan Pages where any business can list their business on one of these pages, add fans and provide content to them.

Once you have created a huge following, you can use your fan page to connect with your customers and prospects through a wide variety of functions such as posting on your "wall", asking them questions or posting up videos, photos and content of interest to your niche.

The best thing is, whenever you post something on your Fan page wall, all the users who "liked" your Fan page will see it on their news updates.

Any actions which a fan takes on the fan page such as post on the wall will be seen by all their friends, so there is huge potential for viral marketing

The fact is this... If you fail to tap into the power of Facebook marketing, you'll potentially be leaving tons of money on the table!

Chapter 3:
Building Your Online Presence Using Fan Pages

Synopsis

So how do you grow your business using Facebook Fan Pages?

Building It

Well, the first thing you must do is sign up for a page. If you already have a Facebook profile, scroll down to the bottom of the page and select "Create A Page".

Once you have created a page, fill in all the necessary details of your business such as contact information, maps, post up a photo of your company logo etc.

The next thing you must do is get your customers and followers onto your Facebook Fan Page. You can do so by encouraging them, whether through email or your website to join and "Like" your Facebook Fan Page.

Getting more fans

Besides asking your existing fan base or email list to join you on Facebook, another option is to advertise using Facebook's advertising system. You can either send them to your Facebook page or send them to your website, but usually sending them to your Facebook page is the cheaper alternative.

What's next?

Once you've got a page set up and a fan base up and running, you should focus on providing targeted, valuable content to your fans. By encouraging them to interact on your page, you create more hype on the page and they would be more likely to share it with their friends, thus getting you more followers.

Chapter 4:
Getting opt ins using Facebook

Synopsis

Have you heard of a landing page or opt in page? Marketers online use them to get leads for their email marketing campaign.

Opt-ins

Did you know that it is possible to set up a "Facebook Landing Page" using Facebook? Search for the "Facebook land page app" and install it in your Facebook Fan Page settings.

Then, you'll have to add in html code into your "before liking" box and "after liking" box. Basically, how a Facebook Landing Page works is you attempt to "bribe" people to "Like" your Facebook page in exchange for access to a free gift.

This free gift could be something like a free e-book or an online video course.

Combine this with your Facebook Advertising funnel, it's like you are typically paying for leads! This can be a quick way to build your list fast and cheap with highly qualified subscribers.

Here's an example of a Facebook Landing Page:

Diagram 1: A non-fan has to "like" your page to get a free gift

Diagram 2: New fan gets instant access to the free gift by entering his name and email (this is your code for the opt in box)

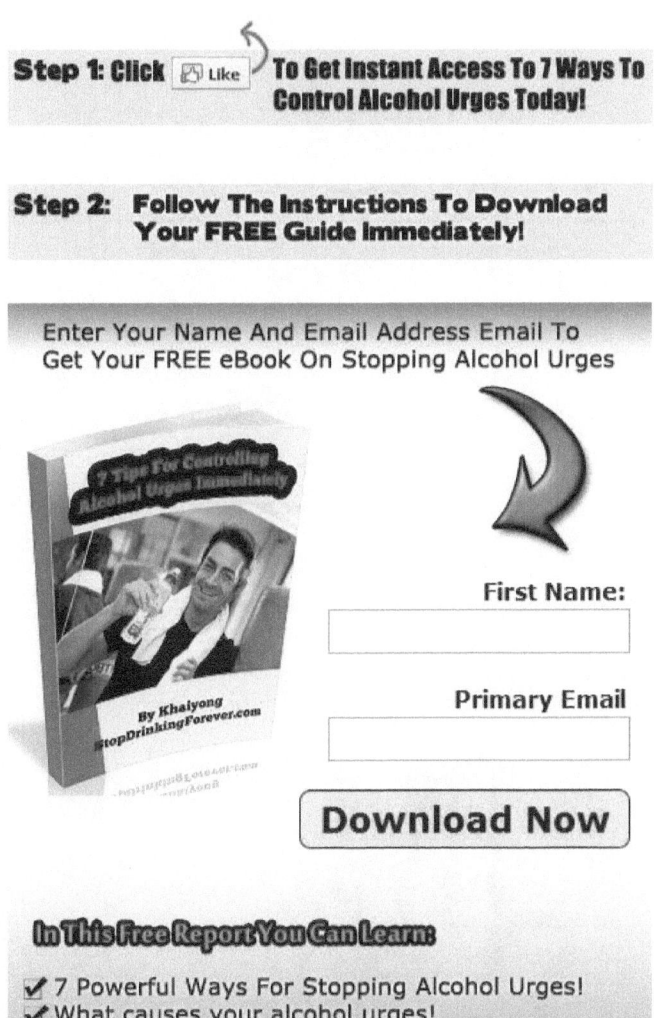

Another simpler way of getting leads fast is simply promoting your landing page on your fan wall, since the fan wall is always the most popular and has a lot of eyeballs; the potential of growing your list fast through there is very big.

Chapter 5:
Viral Power

Synopsis

One of the reasons why Facebook has picked up so fast as the largest and one of the fastest growing websites in the world is because it is viral in nature. Things spread easily via word of mouth with Facebook. That is why many big corporations have recognized this power and have been finding ways to tap into this power.

Going Viral

Whether you are a small business owner or own a huge chain of businesses, you have the potential to tap into the viral nature of Facebook to grow your business rapidly. Here's how:

Every person on Facebook is connected to his or her friends through the network. Status updates of each person such as "Liking" a page, writing on someone's wall will be shown on that person's news feed.

What happens is this – When you get your Facebook fans to interact with your Facebook page, whatever actions they take will be shown on their news feed as well. This in turn would appear on the news feed on all of their friends. This will spark curiosity among their friends and they would be likely to click on your Fan page to see what's going on.

The viral magic happens when more and more people start "Liking" and interacting on your page. Your fan page could grow 10 times the speed in no time!

Chapter 6:
Integrating Facebook With Other Websites

Synopsis

Having tons of Facebook traffic is good, but it won't be of any use unless you get them to your online business websites.

Remember, the Facebook Fan Page serves as an "outpost" for providing useful updates and letting the fans interact with one another. But ultimately, your profits will not directly come from your Facebook traffic unless you know how to monetize them.

Here are some ways you can monetize your Facebook traffic:
1) Send them to your landing page if you don't have a Facebook landing page to build your list of prospects.
2) Promote offers and send them to your sales page.
3) Give excerpts to articles of interest and link the full article to your blog.
4) Ask them to follow you on Twitter and get them to tweet about your content for a prize.
5) Post up videos on YouTube, share them on your Facebook Fan Page and ask them to share it with their friends! (Or subscribe to your YouTube fan page)

So as you can see, The Facebook Fan page acts like a simple hub where all your marketing activities can revolve around it. Ultimately, you have to determine your most desired result (e.g. getting new leads, making profits) and structure your Facebook marketing activities to lead to these sort of responses.

Chapter 7:
Facebook Advertising

Synopsis

Facebook advertising has taken the online marketing world by storm because of its low cost per click and ability to be extremely specific to your target demographics.

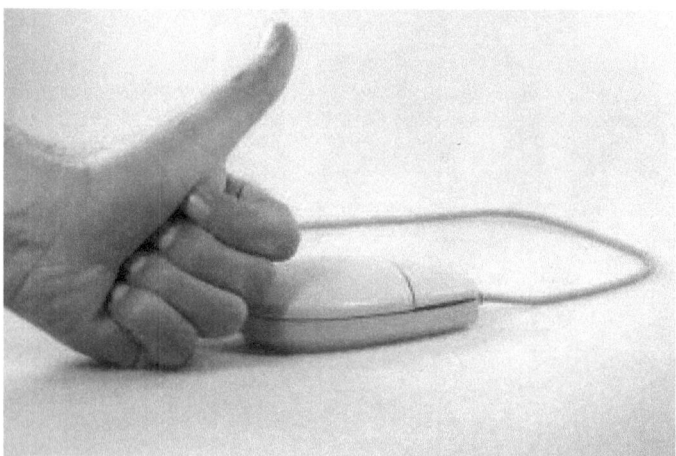

Ads

Its ease of setting up marketing and advertising campaigns allows it to very soon surpass Google in terms of advertising volume.

Setting up your advertising page is simple, at your Facebook profile. First, go to your Facebook page. On the right side there is a mock advertisement, Click it to start crafting your own Advertising campaign to suit your marketing needs.

You can then write your ad copy, include an image and set your marketing budget. Facebook will help you calculate your suggested bid per click based on the average you pay per click.

As a general rule of thumb, you would want to send these clicks to your Facebook landing page so that you can secure leads. If you send them to an external website, it would normally cost more.

After you set up your campaign, you can monitor your advertising statistics and results and tweak your campaign accordingly.

You can adjust your bid, run multiple ad copies to see which converts the best and eliminate those that aren't performing well.

Chapter 8:

Facebook Mistakes To Avoid

Synopsis

With all the so called "hype" about Facebook marketing, it seems imperative that you must tap into this huge resource ASAP. But that being said, there are several pitfalls involved in Facebook marketing that you should be aware of and avoid.

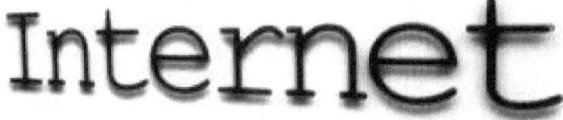

Errors

1) Becoming too "Salesy". This is a big no-no. The main purpose of your Facebook fan page is to connect with your customers and build a strong rapport. Each time you sell them, you take away "rapport juice" and they will become less responsive to your content as time goes by.

2) Not split testing your ads. If you are advertising on Facebook and you don't have multiple ad campaigns to see which converts the best, you'll potential be leaving tons of money on the table. Split test your ads, get rid of those that suck.

3) Not engaging your audience. The amount of success your business will have is not just determined by the number of "likes" you get. You have to turn your audience into raving fans by getting them actively involved in your fan page.

Avoid these mistakes, and you'll be on the path to success.

Wrapping Up

Facebook is the currently the next big online marketing trend, and is unlikely to go out of fashion due to the pace and size at which it is going. This isn't like one of those dot com bubbles which come and go, this is the real deal. 500 Million users can't be wrong.

Due to the competitive nature of the online market, people are constantly looking for new ways to make money and gain new customers. It costs way more to get new customers than to retain existing ones, so Facebook serves a great place to establish rapport with your existing customer or fan base and continue to provide them content of value.

Needless to say, if you fail to tap into the massive marketing powers of Facebook, not only will your competitors rapidly overtake you in terms of market share, you will potentially be leaving tons of money on the table.

That being said, it's time to jump on the Facebook bandwagon before its too late!

To your Facebook Marketing Success!